C. CHRISTOPHER
AND JOHN PATTISON

CULTIVATING **COMMUNITY**
IN THE **PATIENT** WAY OF
JESUS

STUDY GUIDE

Eleven Sessions for Group Discussion

IVP Books

An imprint of InterVarsity Press
Downers Grove, Illinois

InterVarsity Press
P.O. Box 1400, Downers Grove, IL 60515-1426
ivpress.com
email@ivpress.com

InterVarsity Press® is the book-publishing division of InterVarsity Christian Fellowship/USA®, a movement of students and faculty active on campus at hundreds of universities, colleges and schools of nursing in the United States of America, and a member movement of the International Fellowship of Evangelical Students. For information about local and regional activities, visit intervarsity.org.

Scripture quotations, unless otherwise noted, are from the New Revised Standard Version of the Bible, copyright 1989 by the Division of Christian Education of the National Council of the Churches of Christ in the USA. Used by permission. All rights reserved.

While any stories in this book are true, some names and identifying information may have been changed to protect the privacy of individuals.

Cover design: Cindy Kiple
Interior design: Beth McGill
Images: brick wall: jimss/Getty Images
 ivy: © Praiwun/iStockphoto

ISBN 978-0-8308-4130-1 (print)
ISBN 978-0-8308-9426-0 (digital)

Printed in the United States of America ∞

g green
press
ᴵᴺᴵᵀᴵᴬᵀᴵⱽᴱ
As a member of the Green Press Initiative, InterVarsity Press is committed to protecting the environment and to the responsible use of natural resources. To learn more, visit greenpressinitiative.org.

P	20	19	18	17	16	15	14	13	12	11	10	9	8	7	6	5	4	3	2	1
Y	33	32	31	30	29	28	27	26	25	24	23	22	21	20	19	18	17	16		

Contents

How to Use This Study Guide. 5

1 A Theological Vision for Slow Church 10

2 Terroir 14
   Taste and See

3 Stability 18
   Fidelity to People and Place

4 Patience 21
   Entering into the Suffering of Others

5 Wholeness 24
   The Reconciliation of All Things

6 Work 27
   Cooperating with God's Reconciling Mission

7 Sabbath 31
   The Rhythm of Reconciliation

8 Abundance 35
   The Economy of Creation

9 Gratitude 39
   Receiving the Good Gifts of God

10 Hospitality 42
   Generously Sharing God's Abundance

11 Dinner Table Conversation as a Way of
   Being Church 46

How to Use This Study Guide

Publishing a book can feel a lot like preparing a meal without knowing precisely who or how many people will show up, what will bring them or if they will like the food when they taste it. You spend one or two years cooking, likely with a particular kind of guest in mind, trying to be faithful to the ingredients, your tools, your vision and your work. You set the table and send out invitations, and on the day the banquet is ready—release day—you open wide your doors and wait. It's only when the guests start arriving that you begin to get a sense of what they think about what you prepared. You talk to them about the meal and listen to them discuss it with each other. Trust us when we say that the conversation makes it all worthwhile. In fact, it can be thrilling!

When *Slow Church* was first released, we really didn't know what to expect. What happened next has been humbling and surprising and delightful. *Slow Church* has ended up in college classrooms and on the required reading list of major seminaries. It's been published in the United Kingdom and Australia, and there is now a Korean-language version. We've shared the stage with the leadership of Slow Food and Slow Money, and talked about Slow Church at conferences and in churches, living rooms and backyards around North America. A number of early articles and reviews speculated about a "Slow Church

Movement," but our goal has never been to build a movement, only to foster a conversation. However, we see that something is stirring in the church as communities of Jesus followers long to be more faithfully rooted in the place and pace of their neighborhoods.

Much of the Slow Church conversation is happening in small groups, which is fitting. We hope this study guide fulfills the numerous requests we have received for an expanded version of the discussion questions included in the book. Although you should feel free to adapt the guide to fit your own context, here are some recommendations for the components of each session.

READING

This is the reading that all participants will do prior to gathering. Most sessions, this will be only one chapter from the book, although the first and last sessions also include the foreword, introduction and conclusion.

FACILITATOR PREP

For facilitators who want to do some additional preparation (less than an hour per session), we have included several types of resources, including videos and TED Talks, audio recordings and some articles. These should be useful in providing additional context for the material in the book; you might even find some of them worth sharing with your group. We encourage you to pick and choose.

You can find links to these resources on a single landing page on the Slow Church website at guide.slowchurch.com. We'll continue to add more as they become available, and if you come across new resources you think will be helpful for other facilitators, let us know!

WELCOME

Suggested time: 10 minutes

Start your time together with some centering practices, giving everyone a chance to arrive in both body and spirit. This is also a conscious reminder that the goal of the discussion group isn't to get something done as efficiently as possible. The goal is to be present with one another, with God and with our neighbors.

Sit in silence for a few minutes and open with a word of prayer.

Then listen to a song or read a poem. We've included the names and titles of some of our favorites. You'll find links to many of them on our website.

LECTIO DIVINA

Suggested time: 15 minutes

Lectio divina is a centuries-old Christian practice of reading, praying and reflecting on Scripture, often in the context of community. Chris calls it "Slow Reading." As Chris explains in his new book *Reading for the Common Good*, lectio divina is a kind of school where we learn to hear Christ and the word of God, and learn to devote our whole selves to Christ as part of the people of God.

Don't be intimidated by the Latin or its ancient roots. Lectio is as important and relevant as ever, and it's easy to do. The Scripture passage provided will be read three times at a gentle and unhurried pace, preferably by different participants. After the text is read, pause for at least a minute and then ask the following focus questions:

- First reading: What is one word or phrase that touched my heart?

- Second reading: Where does that one word or phrase touch my life today?

- Third reading: What is the text calling *me* to do or become today? What is the text calling *us* to do or become?

CONVERSATION STARTERS

Suggested time: 60 minutes

This study guide includes an expanded list of questions to help keep the conversation going. In our experience, you probably won't need them all since participants will be bringing their own questions and reflections. Although the questions are presented in a sequence that makes sense to us, don't rush to get through them. The discussion will go places no one can predict . . . and that's a good thing!

We suggest beginning the first session by collectively identifying the characteristics of good conversation: vulnerability, confidentiality, listening, assuming the best of each other and so on. Then task someone to craft a set of "agreements" for participants to make with one another. For example, John's church has developed a list of thirteen agreements as they have embraced conversation as a formative practice. The full list is available on our website (guide.slowchurch.com), but it includes the following:

- We will acknowledge Christ's presence among us and in each one of us.

- We will practice reconciliation.

- We will not be afraid of silence.

These agreements are often read out loud, and they are always open to revision.

Finally, find ways to encourage the participation of everyone—including introverts or people who are more deliberate in their processing—by inviting input from folks who haven't had the opportunity to share. It's also wise to consider the difference between reacting and responding. Some groups do this by incorporating pauses and "pulse checks": ask participants to pause for five seconds between comments. Not only does this slow the pace of the discussion but it also gives everyone a chance to process (and honor) what has just been said.

CLOSING THOUGHT

Suggested time: 5 minutes

We have included a final quote as a way of closing your time together. While this can be used to spark one final point of discussion, we envision it as a parting thought for participants to take with them for reflection in the coming week.

Would you mind keeping in touch? We would love to hear about the Slow Church conversations that are happening in your communities. (Actually, we'd even love to pop in via Skype or Google Hangouts to say hello to your group!) We also welcome your suggestions, so we've included both of our personal email addresses below.

More people from more places have come to the Slow Church banquet than we expected. But there is also a sense that the feast is just getting started. In fact, it's turning into a potluck; every new guest is bringing something unique to the table. The two of us are learning so much from you. Thank you!

Chris and John

CONTACT US

C. Christopher Smith: englewoodreview@gmail.com
John Pattison: johnepattison@gmail.com
Twitter: @SlowChurches
guide.slowchurch.com

1

A Theological Vision for Slow Church

READ

- Foreword by Jonathan Wilson-Hartgrove
- Introduction
- Chapter 1: "A Theological Vision for Slow Church"

FACILITATOR PREP

- Slow Food Manifesto
- Carl Honoré, "In praise of slowness" (video)
- David Fitch, "A Slow Church Ecclesiology" (video)

> **These and all other resources are available at guide.slowchurch.com.**

WELCOME

Pierre Teilhard de Chardin, "Trust in the Slow Work of God" (poem)

LECTIO DIVINA

Read the following text with these three questions in mind:

- First reading: What word or phrase touched my heart?
- Second reading: Where does that word or phrase touch my life today?
- Third reading: What is the text calling *me* to do or become? What is the text calling *us* to do or become?

Our firm decision is to work from this focused center: One man died for everyone. That puts everyone in the same boat. He included everyone in his death so that everyone could also be included in his life, a resurrection life, a far better life than people ever lived on their own.

Because of this decision we don't evaluate people by what they have or how they look. We looked at the Messiah that way once and got it all wrong, as you know. We certainly don't look at him that way anymore. Now we look inside, and what we see is that anyone united with the Messiah gets a fresh start, is created new. The old life is gone; a new life burgeons! Look at it! All this comes from the God who settled the relationship between us and him, and then called us to settle our relationships with each other. God put the world square with himself through the Messiah, giving the world a fresh start by offering forgiveness of sins. God has given us the task of telling everyone what he is doing. We're Christ's representatives. God uses us to persuade men and women to drop their differences and enter into God's work of making things right between them. We're speaking for Christ himself now: Become friends with God; he's already a friend with you.

How? you ask. In Christ. God put the wrong on him who never did anything wrong, so we could be put right with God. (2 Cor 5:14-21 *The Message*)

CONVERSATION STARTERS

1. Slow Food, Slow Money, Slow Cities and the other Slow movements differ in scale, scope and strategy. What they have in common is their opposition to what Canadian journalist Carl Honoré describes as "the cult of speed": a philosophy of life that is controlling, aggressive, impatient, etc. What are some ways we have ceded ground to the cult of speed—in life, society, culture and even in the church?

2. *Slow Church* suggests that what makes the Slow movements so compelling is that they make possible "real and meaningful" presence. How does Fast Life threaten to short-circuit real and meaningful presence—with God, with one another, with our own selves and with the natural world?

3. "Many churches . . . come dangerously close to reducing Christianity to a commodity that can be packaged, marketed and sold. Instead of cultivating a deep, holistic discipleship that touches every aspect of our lives, we've confined the life of faith to Sunday mornings, where it can be kept safe and predictable, or to a 'personal relationship with Jesus Christ,' which can be managed from the privacy of our own home. Following Jesus has been diminished to a privatized faith rather than a lifelong apprenticeship undertaken in the context of Christian community" (14). This is flamethrower language. Why do you agree or disagree with this assessment?

4. *Slow Church* was written by nonspecialists (20). Neither author is a pastor, church planter or professional theologian. How do the vocations and gifts of people in your congregation who are not church specialists give shape to your church's life together?

5. No one is a passive observer in the biblical drama. God desires collaboration with humanity, which "undermines our cultural impulse to be consumers and spectators rather than faithful participants in the unwritten fifth act of God's play" (23). What will happen when more people move from being "church consumers" to coproducers of God's Story in the world?

6. "Our calling in Christ is to *community*, to a life shared with others in a local gathering that is an expression of Christ's body in our particular place. The people of God become a sort of demonstration plot for what God intends for all humanity and all creation" (29-30). What are the theological and practical convictions of your congregation that give shape to following together in the way of Jesus?

7. What are the shared practices that help form your congregation as
   a local church community? What are the particular strategic initia-
   tives to which God has called your local congregation, in its particular time and place, in participation with God's mission?

CLOSING THOUGHT

Gerhard Lohfink, *Does God Need the Church? Toward a Theology of the
People of God*:

> It can only be that God begins in a small way, at one single place
> in the world. There must be a place, visible, tangible, where the
> salvation of the world can begin: that is, where the world be-
> comes what it is supposed to be according to God's plan. Be-
> ginning at that place, the new thing can spread abroad, but not
> through persuasion, not through indoctrination, not through
> violence. Everyone must have the opportunity to come and see.
> All must have the chance to behold and test this new thing. Then,
> if they want to, they can allow themselves to be drawn into the
> history of salvation that God is creating. Only in that way can
> their freedom be preserved. What drives them to the new thing
> cannot be force, not even moral pressure, but only the fasci-
> nation of a world that is changed. (27)

2

Terroir

Taste and See

READ

- Chapter 2: "Terroir: Taste and See"

FACILITATOR PREP

- David Fitch's alternative criteria for measuring church success
- Alan Roxburgh, "Why Join God in the Neighborhood?" (video)
- Paul Sparks, Tim Soerens and Dwight Friesen, "The New Parish Movement" (video)

WELCOME

Wendell Berry, "Manifesto: The Mad Farmer Liberation Front" (poem)

LECTIO DIVINA

Then when you pray, GOD will answer.
　You'll call out for help and I'll say, "Here I am."
If you get rid of unfair practices,
　quit blaming victims,
　quit gossiping about other people's sins,
If you are generous with the hungry
　and start giving yourselves to the down-and-out,

Your lives will begin to glow in the darkness,
   your shadowed lives will be bathed in sunlight.
I will always show you where to go.
   I'll give you a full life in the emptiest of places—
   firm muscles, strong bones.
You'll be like a well-watered garden,
   a gurgling spring that never runs dry.
You'll use the old rubble of past lives to build anew,
   rebuild the foundations from out of your past.
You'll be known as those who can fix anything,
   restore old ruins, rebuild and renovate,
   make the community livable again. (Is 58:9-12 *The Message*)

CONVERSATION STARTERS

1. "Slow Church is rooted in the natural, human and spiritual cultures of a particular place. It is a distinctively local expression of the global body of Christ. 'The Word became flesh and blood, and moved into the neighborhood' (Jn 1:14 *The Message*)" (43). What kind of impact could the church's "commitment to place" have on our congregations and neighborhoods?

2. The word *terroir* refers to "the taste of the place." What is the terroir of your neighborhood? Identify a few of the people, places, rhythms and shared beliefs that give your community its unique taste and texture. How can your church celebrate the unique and delicious "flavors" already present in your neighborhood? How can you celebrate these things in ways that do not vainly "puff up" but rather bear witness to the transforming work of God?

3. After reading about the church growth movement, you likely can recognize its influence in your church or churches around you. The scriptural standard for ministry is faithfulness, not numbers, yet the primary metric by which we try to judge the health of our churches is by counting: attendance, tithing, souls saved,

baptisms, etc. What are the alternative measurements of "success"? What are the markers of a healthy, flourishing church? Is it possible to be more narrative driven?

4. The four primary values of McDonaldization are *efficiency, calculability, predictability* and *control*. The book gives examples of how each of these values "have crept into many of our churches, flattening out the flavor of our witness before the watching world" (51). Where have you observed churches that are countering the values of McDonaldization? What are they doing well?

5. The language of experimentation and apprenticeship is used in several places throughout the book. For example: "We find out who Jesus is along the way. We walk the way with Jesus, only to discover that Jesus himself has been the Way and also the destination. Jesus invited people who were skeptical about his teachings to try them on for size: 'Anyone who resolves to do the will of God will know whether the teaching is from God or whether I am speaking on my own' (Jn 7:17)" (56). How comfortable are you with using the language of apprenticeship to describe a life of discipleship? Explain.

6. After a Slow Church event, church leaders often ask, "What do we do next?" While there are many wonderful things churches can do to slow down and become more faithfully present in the place and pace of their neighborhoods, the authors encourage churches to think twice before adding yet another well-intentioned program, practice or activity. Instead, think about the *how* and *why* of what you're *already* doing. Does your church sing, pray and study Scripture together in order to be productive and "get something done"? If so, how can these practices be re-oriented toward deep presence?

7. What things bring the greatest joy to your congregation? Which celebrations are most anticipated each year? Why are they met with great joy, and how did they come to be so?

CLOSING THOUGHT

C. Christopher Smith and John Pattison, *Slow Church: Cultivating Community in the Patient Way of Jesus*:

> We are bound one to another, but a culture built on speed wants to fling us out from the center like a centrifuge. Thus, to commit ourselves to cultivating goodness through practices of nearness and stability, and to conversationally develop shared traditions, is to take a stand against alienation. It is a way of crafting a new, shared story for the community, while connecting us to the cosmic church across time and prefiguring the kingdom of God. It is also an acknowledgement that our fates are wrapped up with the fates of our neighbors. As the prophet Jeremiah wrote in his letter to the exiles, "But seek the welfare of the city where I have sent you into exile, and pray to the LORD on its behalf, for in its welfare you will find your welfare" (Jer 29:7). (43-44)

3

Stability

Fidelity to People and Place

READ

- Chapter 3: "Stability: Fidelity to People and Place"

FACILITATOR PREP

- Jonathan Wilson-Hartgrove, "The Wisdom of Stability for Churches" (video)
- "What Are the Instruments of Good Works?," The Rule of St. Benedict, Chapter IV

WELCOME

Wendell Berry, "A Poem on Hope" (poem)

LECTIO DIVINA

Let love be genuine; hate what is evil, hold fast to what is good; love one another with mutual affection; outdo one another in showing honor. Do not lag in zeal, be ardent in spirit, serve the Lord. Rejoice in hope, be patient in suffering, persevere in prayer. Contribute to the needs of the saints; extend hospitality to strangers.

Bless those who persecute you; bless and do not curse them. Rejoice with those who rejoice, weep with those who weep. Live in harmony with one another; do not be haughty, but associate with the lowly; do not claim to be wiser than you are. Do not repay anyone evil for evil, but take thought for what is noble in the sight of all. If it is possible, so far as it depends on you, live peaceably with all. (Rom 12:9-18)

CONVERSATION STARTERS

1. Where do the members of your church live? What is your church doing (or what could your church be doing) to connect members who live in close proximity? How might members be able to share life together on a daily (or several times a week) basis?

2. What is the story of your church? Have you always existed in your current location? If not, where were you located before, why did you move, and what were the effects of your move on the church and the former neighborhood? If you have always been in your current location, have there been times when the church was tempted to move, and what factors led to the decision to stay?

3. Where are the third places—neither home nor work—where people gather in your neighborhood? Are there members of your congregation regularly engaged in those places? How can they build stronger bridges between your church and the neighborhood? What are ways that you can engage more in third places?

4. What practices does your church have of listening to your neighbors? How are the members of your church encouraged to be attentive to their neighbors? How is your church involved in neighborhood efforts? (By neighborhood efforts, we mean an event or program organized primarily by those outside the church, not a church-run program that neighbors are invited into.)

5. Pick a radius appropriate for your context (shorter for urban places, longer for rural) and identify all the churches within that radius. How have you connected or collaborated with those

congregations? If you haven't, how can you connect and move in the direction of collaboration?

6. How many people leave your congregation in a given year? Is there any recognition of their leaving? What conversational practices do you have (or could you develop) for helping people discern whether they should stay or leave your congregation?

7. How many addresses have you lived at in the last ten years? How many major moves were involved—from one city, state or country to another? What were the reasons for moving? What are the positives and negatives of having moved (or not moved) so frequently?

8. What things do you do (or could you do) to get to know and appreciate your neighbors better? Are there things you are already doing—exercising (walking/running/biking), eating out, going out for coffee, etc.—that you could do in your neighborhood?

CLOSING THOUGHT

C. Christopher Smith and John Pattison, *Slow Church: Cultivating Community in the Patient Way of Jesus*:

> God is transforming creation. If we slow down and stay put long enough, we too will be changed into the likeness of Christ. The scope of our vision will also be changed. Instead of speaking in broad generalities about changing the world, we will find ourselves free to imagine in more specific ways the transformation of our own particular places. We can trust that God is orchestrating the renewal of all creation and that God will raise up people in other places who will care for those places as much as we care for ours. (74)

4

Patience

Entering into the Suffering of Others

READ

- Chapter 4: "Patience: Entering into the Suffering of Others"

FACILITATOR PREP

- "Crash Course World History: The Industrial Revolution" (video)
- Renovaré, "The Jesus Way Conference Preview" (video)

WELCOME

Over the Rhine, "All I Need Is Everything" (song)

LECTIO DIVINA

Thomas said to him, "Lord, we do not know where you are going. How can we know the way?" Jesus said to him, "I am the way, and the truth, and the life. No one comes to the Father except through me. If you know me, you will know my Father also. From now on you do know him and have seen him."

Philip said to him, "Lord, show us the Father, and we will be satisfied." Jesus said to him, "Have I been with you all this time, Philip, and you still do not know me? Whoever has seen me has seen the Father. How can you say, 'Show us the Father'? Do you not believe that I am in the Father and the Father is in me? The words that I say to you I do not speak on my own; but the Father who dwells in me does his works. Believe me that I am in the Father and the Father is in me; but if you do not, then believe me because of the works themselves." (Jn 14:5-11)

CONVERSATION STARTERS

1. In what sorts of situations do you find yourself most impatient? Why are you impatient, and how do you deal with your impatience?

2. To what extent do we question the technology of our age and its effects on our lives? Describe some ways in which technology has made you more impatient. Are there ways in which a particular technology has made you more patient, or has cultivated some other virtue in you?

3. Reflect on a time when your church acted impatiently as a congregation. What was driving the impatience? What were the outcomes of the impatient action, and what would you do differently if you were faced with a similar situation now?

4. What are the things that you believe are worth pursuing (or protecting) "by any means necessary"? Why?

5. If Jesus is not only the person that we are to embody together in our neighborhood but also the way in which we are to do so, then we need to better understand who he is. What did he teach? How did he live? And how are these questions related?

6. What practices of confession does your church have? When has that practice worked well and benefited the health and well-being of your congregation?

7. In what ways does your church enter into the sufferings of others in your church or neighborhood? When you have failed to enter into (or failed to fully enter into) the sufferings of others?

8. In *The Jesus Way*, Eugene Peterson says, "A Christian congregation, the church in your neighborhood, has always been the primary

location for getting this *way* and *truth* and *life* of Jesus believed and embodied" (92). If Peterson is right, what might this mean for the ways in which we share life together?

CLOSING THOUGHT

C. Christopher Smith and John Pattison, *Slow Church: Cultivating Community in the Patient Way of Jesus*:

> The local church is the crucible in which we are forged as the patient people of God. We have been united with each other in the life, death, resurrection and ascension of Jesus. As we mature together into the fullness of Christ (Eph 4:13), over time and in our places, we learn patience by forgiving and being reconciled to one another. Our brothers and sisters may incessantly annoy us. But we are called in Christ to love and to be reconciled to them. Just as marriage vows serve as a covenant bond that holds a couple together in difficult times, our commitment to our faith community is essential if we are to learn patience and practice stability. Patience can hold us together when other forces conspire to rip us asunder. (87)

5

Wholeness

The Reconciliation of All Things

READ

- Chapter 5: "Wholeness: The Reconciliation of All Things"

FACILITATOR PREP

- Howard A. Snyder, preface and introduction, *Salvation Means Creation Healed*

- Jo Bailey Wells, "On the Psalms of Lament and Resources for Healing" (video)

- Parker Palmer on Clearness Committees (video)

WELCOME

Liberty Hyde Bailey, "Brotherhood" (poem)

LECTIO DIVINA

He is the image of the invisible God, the firstborn of all creation; for in him all things in heaven and on earth were created, things visible and invisible, whether thrones or dominions or rulers or powers—all things have been created through him and for him. He himself is before all things, and in him all things hold together. He is the head of the body, the church; he is the beginning, the firstborn from the dead, so that he might come to have first place in everything. For in him all the fullness of God was pleased to dwell, and through him God was pleased to reconcile to himself all things, whether on earth or in heaven, by making peace through the blood of his cross.

And you who were once estranged and hostile in mind, doing evil deeds, he has now reconciled in his fleshly body through death, so as to present you holy and blameless and irreproachable before him—provided that you continue securely established and steadfast in the faith, without shifting from the hope promised by the gospel that you heard, which has been proclaimed to every creature under heaven. I, Paul, became a servant of this gospel. (Col 1:15-23)

CONVERSATION STARTERS

1. Name the fragmentations that exist in your congregation. Race? Age? Economic class? Political party? Where can people on either side of any of these divides actively engage with those on the opposite side—talking and working together and knowing each other first and foremost as brothers and sisters in Christ? How can you nurture more of these opportunities for healing and reconciliation to begin?

2. Name the fragmentations that exist in your neighborhood. Race? Age? Economic class? Political party? Where can neighbors on either side of any of these divides actively engage with those on the opposite side—talking and working together and knowing each other first and foremost as neighbors who share together in this place? Are there ways you can nurture more of these opportunities?

3. Howard Snyder describes creation as an interconnected whole in which "everything is related to everything else" (102). Do you agree? Why or why not? What are some implications of this perspective on the interconnectedness of creation for the Christian life?

4. What are some ways in which we think and act dualistically as churches and individuals, dividing life up into spiritual and material/secular? What are the effects of our dualism?

5. Is there any group of people that you would say is not welcome in your church? Why?

6. If your church has any practices of lament, share about a time when you lamented together. What were you lamenting? What happened as a result of the lament?

7. What is your congregational process for decision making? How do you ensure that as many people as possible can speak into the decision-making process if they so desire?

8. How carefully do you examine the impact your decisions might have on your neighbors? On other churches? On the land or creation as a whole? Are there ways for people outside your congregation, who might have wisdom pertinent to a particular decision, to speak into your decisions?

CLOSING THOUGHT

The Constitution of the Iroquois Nations:

> In all your efforts at law making, in all your official acts, self-interest shall be cast into oblivion. . . . Look and listen for the welfare of the whole people and have always in view not only the present but also the coming generations, even those whose faces are yet beneath the surface of the ground—the unborn of the future nation.

6

Work

Cooperating with God's Reconciling Mission

READ

- Chapter 6: "Work: Cooperating with God's Reconciling Mission"

FACILITATOR PREP

- This Is Our City, *Christianity Today* (videos)
- Redeeming Work Conferences, *Leadership Journal* (videos)

WELCOME

Dorothy Sayers, "Why Work?":

> [The Church] has allowed work and religion to become separate departments, and is astonished to find that, as result, the secular work of the world is turned to purely selfish and destructive ends, and that the greater part of the world's intelligent workers have become irreligious, or at least, uninterested in religion.
>
> But is it astonishing? How can anyone remain interested in a religion which seems to have no concern with nine-tenths of his life? The Church's approach to an intelligent carpenter is usually confined to exhorting him not to be drunk and disorderly in his leisure hours, and to come to church on Sundays. What the Church should be telling him is this: that the very first demand that his religion makes upon him is that he should make good tables.

Church by all means, and decent forms of amusement, certainly—but what use is all that if in the very center of his life and occupation he is insulting God with bad carpentry? No crooked table legs or ill-fitting drawers ever, I dare swear, came out of the carpenter's shop at Nazareth. Nor, if they did, could anyone believe that they were made by the same hand that made Heaven and earth. No piety in the worker will compensate for work that is not true to itself; for any work that is untrue to its own technique is a living lie.

LECTIO DIVINA

For I am about to create new heavens
   and a new earth;
the former things shall not be remembered
   or come to mind.
But be glad and rejoice forever
   in what I am creating;
for I am about to create Jerusalem as a joy,
   and its people as a delight.
I will rejoice in Jerusalem,
   and delight in my people;
no more shall the sound of weeping be heard in it,
   or the cry of distress.
No more shall there be in it
   an infant that lives but a few days,
   or an old person who does not live out a lifetime;
for one who dies at a hundred years will be considered a youth,
   and one who falls short of a hundred will be considered
      accursed.
They shall build houses and inhabit them;
   they shall plant vineyards and eat their fruit.
They shall not build and another inhabit;
   they shall not plant and another eat;

for like the days of a tree shall the days of my people be,
    and my chosen shall long enjoy the work of their hands.
They shall not labor in vain,
    or bear children for calamity;
for they shall be offspring blessed by the LORD—
    and their descendants as well.
Before they call I will answer,
    while they are yet speaking I will hear.
The wolf and the lamb shall feed together,
    the lion shall eat straw like the ox;
    but the serpent—its food shall be dust!
They shall not hurt or destroy
    on all my holy mountain,
      says the LORD. (Is 65:17-25)

CONVERSATION STARTERS

1. What was the first job that you really loved? What did you love about it?

2. "Work is such a complex, important and even intimate part of what it means to be human that it's surprising how little the American church has had to say about it in recent decades" (123). Does your church talk about work, in all its complexity and ambiguity? If so, what is the conversation?

3. Do you see your work—whether paid or unpaid—as a calling? What is your theology of work and how has it changed over time?

4. Describe a work experience you had that was alienating. Describe a work experience you had that was deeply satisfying.

5. Do you think there is a connection between a "rationalized operating manual like the McDonald's 'Bible'" (132) and the way some people approach the actual Bible? Which metaphors for the Scripture are you comfortable with—operating manual, roadmap, GPS, compass, etc.—and why?

6. What are some of the work-related injustices in your community? What should be the response of the church? What are some practical ways the neighborhood church can begin to reclaim work as an expression and instrument of God's *shalom*?

7. What gifts and skills do people in your congregation have that they are willing to make available for the reconciling work of the kingdom? How can you connect people with particular skills to benefit your neighborhood?

8. What spaces does your church have in its life together for people to talk about and reflect theologically on the work they do? How does your congregation strengthen the bonds between the daily work of your members and the mission of the church in your place?

CLOSING THOUGHT

Thomas Merton, *No Man Is an Island*:

> All vocations are intended by God to manifest His love in the world. For each special calling gives a man some particular place in the Mystery of Christ, gives him something to do for the salvation of all mankind. The difference between the various vocations lies in the different ways in which each one enables men to discover God's love, appreciate it, respond to it, and share it with other men. Each vocation has for its aim the propagation of divine life in the world. (162)

7

Sabbath

The Rhythm of Reconciliation

READ

- Chapter 7: "Sabbath: The Rhythm of Reconciliation"

FACILITATOR PREP

- Eugene H. Peterson, "Prayer Time," *Working the Angles*
- Norman Wirzba, "A Sabbath Way to Lead"
- Wendell Berry, *This Day: Collected & New Sabbath Poems*
- Sabbath Manifesto

WELCOME

Wendell Berry, "I go among trees and sit still" (poem)

LECTIO DIVINA

A Psalm. A Song for the Sabbath Day.

> It is good to give thanks to the LORD,
> 	to sing praises to your name, O Most High;
> to declare your steadfast love in the morning,
> 	and your faithfulness by night,
> to the music of the lute and the harp,
> 	to the melody of the lyre.

For you, O Lord, have made me glad by your work;
    at the works of your hands I sing for joy.

How great are your works, O Lord!
    Your thoughts are very deep!
The dullard cannot know,
    the stupid cannot understand this:
though the wicked sprout like grass
    and all evildoers flourish,
they are doomed to destruction forever,
    but you, O Lord, are on high forever.
For your enemies, O Lord,
    for your enemies shall perish;
    all evildoers shall be scattered.

But you have exalted my horn like that of the wild ox;
    you have poured over me fresh oil.
My eyes have seen the downfall of my enemies;
    my ears have heard the doom of my evil assailants.

The righteous flourish like the palm tree,
    and grow like a cedar in Lebanon.
They are planted in the house of the Lord;
    they flourish in the courts of our God.
In old age they still produce fruit;
    they are always green and full of sap,
showing that the Lord is upright;
    he is my rock, and there is no unrighteousness in him. (Ps 92)

CONVERSATION STARTERS

1. "Sabbath is an obvious rebuke to culture—and even a church culture!—that prides itself on its busyness" (141). What are the temptations of busyness for churches? For your church?

2. Sabbath, when it is kept at all, is usually observed as a personal

practice. How can your church or small group practice the sabbath together? What practices do you have of pausing and reflecting together on who God is, who you are and how you are being called to follow in God's mission? If your church doesn't have any shared sabbath practices, what small steps can you take together in this direction?

3. The economics of sabbath compel us to ask ourselves tough questions about *enough*. What does enough look like for your family? For your church? In what area of life could you experiment with sabbath economics? (143)

4. Are there places in your life together where you can transparently discuss your finances—as individuals, as families, as a church—as you strive toward understanding what it means to have enough?

5. The word *redistribution* is a politically charged one, and yet that is what seems to be going on in the economies of Egypt, the wilderness and the early church in Acts. Why are we uncomfortable with the concept of redistribution?

   Sabbath is not just about rest. It's about delight. What is your answer to Dan Allender's question: "What would I do for a twenty-four-hour period of time if the only criteria was to pursue my deepest joy?" What is it about the pursuit of joy and delight that make us feel uneasy? (147)

6. Sabbath trust—"seven days of prosperity for six days work"—was so integral to what it meant to be a part of God's chosen people that the Israelites were instructed to keep a jarful of manna in the ark of the covenant, an ever-present reminder of God's love and provision. What is the "manna" for your church, and what is your "jar"? In other words, how does your church recognize and then memorialize God's abundant provision? Or what are ways you can help your church develop this practice?

CLOSING THOUGHT

Andy Crouch, "Why Should I Observe the Sabbath?," The High Calling:

> Of the Ten Commandments, the longest commandment is the one that begins, "Remember the sabbath and keep it holy." And it's long, because it goes on to talk about all the other people you have to make sure honor the sabbath along with you. Not just you, but your children; not just your family, but the people who work for you; not just the people who work for you, but any foreigners who are residents in the place where you live. God cares about sabbath. It's interesting that the God who made us to work makes the command *not* to work. We are not machines; we're creatures. And the sabbath reminds us that we're creatures who need to rest. One of the tragedies of our culture is that we've lost this. So now we just have to choose it. It's no longer just sort of part of the fabric of our world that things stop on Sundays. Now we have to stop, and it's the best thing you can possibly do if you want to be an image-bearer who contributes to the world.

8

Abundance

The Economy of Creation

READ

- Chapter 8: "Abundance: The Economy of Creation"

FACILITATOR PREP

- Walter Brueggemann, "The Liturgy of Abundance, the Myth of Scarcity"
- William T. Cavanaugh, "When Enough Is Enough"
- Christine Pohl, "An Economy of Gratitude and Hospitality," 2014 Slow Church Conference at Englewood Christian Church.

WELCOME

Gerhard Lohfink, *Does God Need the Church?*:

> God is overflowing life itself, and . . . God's whole desire is to share that life. God's love is beyond all measure, and God's gifts to human beings are not measured by their good behavior.
>
> Hence, the principle of superfluity is evident even in creation itself. Biologists long ago noticed that quantitative and qualitative waste play a role in nature. . . . Nature "luxuriates." What an opulence of flowers and butterflies alone! What a superfluity of seeds to produce a single living thing! What an expenditure of solar systems, Milky Ways, and spiral nebulae! An entire

universe is squandered in order to produce more and more costly forms of life on a *single* planet and to provide a place for the human spirit. (149)

LECTIO DIVINA

Bless the LORD, O my soul.
　　O LORD my God, you are very great.
You are clothed with honor and majesty,
　　wrapped in light as with a garment.
You stretch out the heavens like a tent,
　　you set the beams of your chambers on the waters,
you make the clouds your chariot,
　　you ride on the wings of the wind,
you make the winds your messengers,
　　fire and flame your ministers.

You set the earth on its foundations,
　　so that it shall never be shaken. . . .

O LORD, how manifold are your works!
　　In wisdom you have made them all;
　　the earth is full of your creatures.
Yonder is the sea, great and wide,
　　creeping things innumerable are there,
　　living things both small and great.
There go the ships,
　　and Leviathan that you formed to sport in it.

These all look to you
　　to give them their food in due season;
when you give to them, they gather it up;
　　when you open your hand, they are filled with good things.
When you hide your face, they are dismayed;
　　when you take away their breath, they die
　　and return to their dust.

When you send forth your spirit, they are created;
and you renew the face of the ground.

May the glory of the LORD endure forever;
may the LORD rejoice in his works—
who looks on the earth and it trembles,
who touches the mountains and they smoke.
I will sing to the LORD as long as I live;
I will sing praise to my God while I have being.
May my meditation be pleasing to him,
for I rejoice in the LORD. (Ps 104:1-5, 24-34)

CONVERSATION STARTERS

1. Read the story of the feast that Jesus provided for the crowd of five thousand (Mk 6:30-44) and our interpretation of it (165-67). How do these readings compare with how you have heard the story in the past? Why is this Gospel story important for the church?

2. Tell of a time that you didn't want to be generous. What was the rationale behind your inclination not to be generous?

3. In what ways do you see the economy of scarcity—that there are not enough resources to go around—at work in the world? In your neighborhood? In your congregation?

4. "I came that they may have life, and have it abundantly" (Jn 10:10). What are some ways that God has provided abundantly for the flourishing of your church community?

5. Are there ways in which your church is withholding resources from members or neighbors?

6. What resources do your church members have—the gifts and skills—that could be leveraged to benefit the well-being of your congregation or your neighbors? Pay particular attention to the gifts of those that we tend to marginalize: the young (children and youth) and the old, those with physical or emotional challenges, etc.

7. In what ways could your church make its building and land available for use to benefit members or neighbors?

CLOSING THOUGHT

Walter Brueggemann, "The Liturgy of Abundance, the Myth of Scarcity":

> We who are now the richest nation are today's main coveters. We never feel that we have enough; we have to have more and more, and this insatiable desire destroys us. Whether we are liberal or conservative Christians, we must confess that the central problem of our lives is that we are torn apart by the conflict between our attraction to the good news of God's abundance and the power of our belief in scarcity—a belief that makes us greedy, mean and unneighborly. We spend our lives trying to sort out that ambiguity.
>
> The conflict between the narratives of abundance and of scarcity is the defining problem confronting us at the turn of the millennium. The gospel story of abundance asserts that we originated in the magnificent, inexplicable love of a God who loved the world into generous being. The baptismal service declares that each of us has been miraculously loved into existence by God. And the story of abundance says that our lives will end in God, and that this well-being cannot be taken from us. In the words of St. Paul, neither life nor death nor angels nor principalities nor things—nothing can separate us from God.
>
> What we know about our beginnings and our endings, then, creates a different kind of present tense for us. We can live according to an ethic whereby we are not driven, controlled, anxious, frantic or greedy, precisely because we are sufficiently at home and at peace to care about others as we have been cared for. (343)

9

Gratitude

Receiving the Good Gifts of God

READ

- Chapter 9: "Gratitude: Receiving the Good Gifts of God"

FACILITATOR PREP

- David Steindl-Rast, "Want to Be Happy? Be Grateful" (video)
- Tim Soerens, "Gratitude as Resistance: An Ancient Idea for Our Collective Anxiety," *Sojourners Magazine*
- Jim Diers on the Seven Principles of Asset-Based Community Development (video)
- Introduction to Appreciative Inquiry (video)

WELCOME

Mary Oliver, "Messenger" (poem)

LECTIO DIVINA

Here there is no Gentile or Jew, circumcised or uncircumcised, barbarian, Scythian, slave or free, but Christ is all, and is in all.

Therefore, as God's chosen people, holy and dearly loved, clothe yourselves with compassion, kindness, humility, gentleness and patience. Bear with each other and forgive one another if any of you has a grievance against someone. Forgive as the Lord forgave you. And over all these virtues put on love, which binds them all together in perfect unity.

Let the peace of Christ rule in your hearts, since as members of one body you were called to peace. And be thankful. Let the message of Christ dwell among you richly as you teach and admonish one another with all wisdom through psalms, hymns, and songs from the Spirit, singing to God with gratitude in your hearts. And whatever you do, whether in word or deed, do it all in the name of the Lord Jesus, giving thanks to God the Father through him. (Col 3:11-17 NIV)

CONVERSATION STARTERS

1. What are some practices of gratitude in your church community? How is gratitude expressed to God? How is gratitude expressed to one another?

2. What are your practices of celebration? How do you "rejoice with those who rejoice"?

3. Think back over your history in the congregation. Describe a time when you felt most alive and energized. Who was involved, what happened, and why was it energizing to you?

4. What is the most life-giving virtue of your congregation? How is that virtue evidenced in your congregation?

5. The story of Scripture is the gathering of a people who will make God's goodness known to the world. What are some ways your congregation makes God's goodness known to your neighbors?

6. The book mentions several practices that help churches (and their neighbors) focus more on what is *present* rather than on what is *lacking*. These include asset-mapping in congregations, creating an

asset map of your neighborhoods and exploring appreciative inquiry. Which of these practices resonated with you? Why?

7. "Dissatisfaction is at the very root of our modern economy . . . [and] at the root of a staggering amount of injustice" (180, 182). How is that dissatisfaction perpetuated? What is the counter-message of the church?

8. How can you build gratitude and celebration into the rhythm of your congregational life?

CLOSING THOUGHT

Thomas Merton, *Thoughts in Solitude*:

> Gratitude, though, is more than a mental exercise, more than a formula of words. We cannot be satisfied to make a mental note of things which God has done for us and then perfunctorily thank Him for favors received.
>
> To be grateful is to recognize the Love of God in everything He has given us—and he has given us everything. Every breath we draw is a gift of His love, every moment of existence is a grace, for it brings with it immense graces from Him. Gratitude therefore takes nothing for granted, is never unresponsive, is constantly awakening to new wonder and to praise of the goodness of God. For the grateful man knows that God is good, not by hearsay but by experience. And that is what makes all the difference. (33)

10

Hospitality

Generously Sharing God's Abundance

READ

- Chapter 10: "Hospitality: Generously Sharing God's Abundance"

FACILITATOR PREP

- Interview with Christine Pohl, "Grace Enters with the Stranger" (video/text)
- Elizabeth Newman, *Untamed Hospitality*
- Jean Vanier, "Belonging" (video)

WELCOME

Jean Vanier, *Befriending the Stranger*:

> In the midst of all the violence and corruption of the world God invites us today to create new places of belonging, places of sharing, of peace and of kindness, places where no-one needs to defend himself or herself; places where each one is loved and accepted with one's own fragility, abilities and disabilities. This is my vision for our churches: *that they become places of belonging, places of sharing.* (12)

LECTIO DIVINA

He said also to the one who had invited him, "When you give a luncheon or a dinner, do not invite your friends or your brothers or your relatives or rich neighbors, in case they may invite you in return, and you would be repaid. But when you give a banquet, invite the poor, the crippled, the lame, and the blind. And you will be blessed, because they cannot repay you, for you will be repaid at the resurrection of the righteous."

One of the dinner guests, on hearing this, said to him, "Blessed is anyone who will eat bread in the kingdom of God!" Then Jesus said to him, "Someone gave a great dinner and invited many. At the time for the dinner he sent his slave to say to those who had been invited, 'Come; for everything is ready now.' But they all alike began to make excuses. The first said to him, 'I have bought a piece of land, and I must go out and see it; please accept my regrets.' Another said, 'I have bought five yoke of oxen, and I am going to try them out; please accept my regrets.' Another said, 'I have just been married, and therefore I cannot come.' So the slave returned and reported this to his master. Then the owner of the house became angry and said to his slave, 'Go out at once into the streets and lanes of the town and bring in the poor, the crippled, the blind, and the lame.' And the slave said, 'Sir, what you ordered has been done, and there is still room.' Then the master said to the slave, 'Go out into the roads and lanes, and compel people to come in, so that my house may be filled. For I tell you, none of those who were invited will taste my dinner.'" (Lk 14:12-24)

CONVERSATION STARTERS

1. What are your practices of hospitality as a congregation? How do you make people feel welcome and like they belong to your church

community—particularly people who are outside the typical demographics of your congregation?

2. Who are the "strangers" in your neighborhood, those people who are neglected by the mainstream of culture? Where do they live and spend time? Why are they neglected?

3. In what ways does your church extend hospitality to neighbors who might never attend a church service or activity?

4. In what ways does your congregation demonstrate and encourage generosity? What are some areas in which you might be more generous in the future?

5. Does the church allow neighborhood groups to use its facilities? Share stories of extending hospitality to neighbors, and discuss what you have learned from these experiences.

6. In what ways are resources—homes, cars, skills, tools, etc.—shared among members of your congregation? How can you encourage and facilitate more sharing of resources?

7. Practically speaking, what is it that prevents us from inviting people into our homes?

8. Hospitality requires vulnerability, as the host and guest open themselves up to each other. What are hindrances to vulnerability? How can you cultivate a spirit of vulnerability in your church?

CLOSING THOUGHT

Christine Pohl, "Hospitality, a Practice and Way of Life," in *Vision: A Journal for Church and Theology*:

> Besides sharing food and drink with someone, which is central to almost every act of hospitality, the most important practice of welcome is giving a person our full attention. It is impossible to overstate the significance of paying attention, listening to people's stories, and taking time to talk with them. For those of us

who feel that time is our scarcest resource, often this requires slowing ourselves down sufficiently to be present to the person. It means that we view individuals as human beings rather than as embodied needs or interruptions. Hospitality can be inconvenient and we must be careful not to be grudging in our welcome. It is possible to invite someone in but also to communicate to them "in a thousand small ways" that we have other things we need to be doing, or that we are making a substantial sacrifice to be with them. Obviously we cannot give any one person unlimited amounts of undivided attention, but often we are distracted and some of us pride ourselves on the number of things we can do simultaneously.

Dinner Table Conversation as a Way of Being Church

READ

- Chapter 11: "Dinner Table Conversation as a Way of Being Church"
- Conclusion

FACILITATOR PREP

- Michael Pollan, *Cooked* (7-10)
- Intro to St. Lydia's Dinner Church (video)
- Dan Merica, "Washington Gridlock Linked to Social Funk"
- John Howard Yoder, "Disciples Break Bread Together," *Body Politics*

WELCOME

Joy Harjo, "Perhaps the World Ends Here" (poem)

LECTIO DIVINA

[The Christians in Jerusalem] devoted themselves to the apostles' teaching and fellowship, to the breaking of bread and the prayers.

Awe came upon everyone, because many wonders and signs were being done by the apostles. All who believed were together and had all things in common; they would sell their possessions and goods and distribute the proceeds to all, as any had need.

Day by day, as they spent much time together in the temple, they broke bread at home and ate their food with glad and generous hearts, praising God and having the goodwill of all the people. And day by day the Lord added to their number those who were being saved. (Acts 2:42-47)

CONVERSATION STARTERS

1. Reflect on your childhood experiences of eating together (or not eating together) as a family. What are your most vivid memories of mealtime?

2. What practices of eating together does your church have? How is the food provided for those meals? Who prepares the meal? Who cleans up after the meal? How can you draw more people into the practice of eating together and especially into the work that those meals require?

3. What practices does your church have of sharing meals with neighbors? How could your congregation encourage this practice more broadly?

4. "If we are eating and conversing eucharistically, we imitate Christ in denying ourselves and our own personal agendas" (216). To what extent are your interactions with your fellow church members guided by the eucharistic way of Jesus? What about your interactions with your neighbors? What disciplines are you undertaking to learn to interact in this way?

5. What spaces does your congregation have for open conversation? How do you gently invite more people into those spaces—especially those who might be wary of conversation? If you have multiple spaces for conversation, to what extent are they in harmony? And if they do not fit together harmoniously, what can you do to make them more so?

6. What practices of discernment does your congregation have? For individuals? For the community as a whole? When has discernment

worked well in your church community, or when hasn't discernment worked well?

7. What are some practical ways in which your church community might begin to slow down and recognize the ways in which God is already at work in your church, your homes and your neighborhood?

CLOSING THOUGHT

C. Christopher Smith and John Pattison, *Slow Church: Cultivating Community in the Patient Way of Jesus*:

The extraordinary thing about Slow Church is how ordinary it is. Slow Church is just church—or it should be. We aren't asking people to be Super Christians, to move to a developing nation or to the inner city, or to give away all their money. What we're advocating is that we live more deeply into the ordinary patterns of our lives, considering and talking with others in our church about *how* and *why* we do the things we do.

Slow Church reflects our own longing to experience the subversive, transforming power of God within the day-to-day life of our churches and neighborhoods. The adjectives *subversive* and *transforming* are intentional here, because we are withdrawing our allegiance to a McDonaldized religion that wants to keep the life of faith segmented to Sunday morning services. In a world where God is at work reconciling all creation, everything matters: work, family, friends, place, rest, food, money and, above all, the body of Christ, because the church is the interpretive community through which we make sense of all other facets of life. (223)